REVISED AND UPDATED

Transport Around the World

Motorbikes

Chris Oxlade

BRACKNELL FOREST
BOROUGH COUNCIL

Heinemann
LIBRARY

H www.heinemann.co.uk
Visit our website to find out more information about Heinemann Library books.

To order:
☎ Phone 44 (0) 1865 888066
▤ Send a fax to 44 (0) 1865 314091
💻 Visit the Heinemann Bookshop at www.heinemann.co.uk to browse our catalogue and order online.

First published in Great Britain by Heinemann Library,
Halley Court, Jordan Hill, Oxford OX2 8EJ, part of Harcourt Education.
Heinemann is a registered trademark of Harcourt Education Ltd.

Editorial: Diyan Leake and Kristen Truhlar
Design: Kimberley R. Miracle and Ray Hendren
Picture research: Erica Martin
Production: Julie Carter

Originated by Chroma Graphics (Overseas) Pte Ltd
Printed and bound in China by South China Printing Co. Ltd

ISBN 978 0 4310 8699 6

12 11 10 09 08
10 9 8 7 6 5 4 3 2 1

British Library Cataloguing in Publication Data
Oxlade, Chris
Transport Around the World: Motorbikes

A full catalogue record for this book is available from the British Library

Acknowledgements
The publishers would like to thank the following for permission to reproduce photographs: R.D. Battersby pp. **4**, **6**, **15**, **17**, **23**; Corbis pp. **12** (Reuters), **27** (Zefa/Jon Feingersh); Eye Ubiquitous p. **20**; Getty Images p. **13** (The Image Bank/Moritz Steiger); PA Photos p. **29**; PhotoEdit p. **24** (Dennis MacDonald); Pictures p. **25**; Quadrant pp. **9**, **11**, **14**, **18**, **21**, **22**, **26**; Science and Society Picture Library p. **8**; Tony Stone Images p. **19**; Travel Ink p. **28** (Tim Lynch); TRH Pictures pp. **5** (Gilera), **7**, **10**, **16**.

Cover photograph of a motocross rider reproduced with permission of Getty Images (Jim Arbogast).

The publishers would like to thank Carrie Reiling for her assistance in the publication of this book.

Every effort has been made to contact copyright holders of any material reproduced in this book. Any omissions will be rectified in subsequent printings if notice is given to the publishers.

Contents

Some words are shown in bold, **like this**. You can find out what they mean by looking in the glossary.

What is a motorcycle?

A motorcycle is a machine with an **engine** that moves along on two or three wheels. There is a seat for a rider and sometimes for a passenger too. People use motorcycles to go to work or just for fun.

engine

A motorcycle does not need a lot of space to park.

helmets

handlebars

These riders are enjoying safely riding their motorcycle.

The rider steers a motorcycle to the left or right using the handlebars. Controls on the handlebars make it go faster or slower. The rider should always wear a crash helmet for safety.

How motorcycles work

Most motorcycles have two wheels. Each wheel has a **rubber tyre** around it. The tyres grip the road and stop the motorcycle sliding sideways as it goes round corners.

The wide tyres on a motorcycle help to make it safe to ride.

tyre

This is the rear wheel
of a motorcycle.

A motorcycle has an **engine** that makes the rear
wheel turn. It is connected to the wheel with a
chain. The engine needs **fuel** to make it work.

Old motorcycles

This strange machine was one of the first motorcycles.

One of the first motorcycles was built in 1885 in Germany. It had a wooden frame and wooden wheels. Today's motorcycles are mostly made of metal and plastic.

This motorcycle is called the
Silent Grey Fellow.

Around 1900, companies began making motorcycles for people to buy. One of these motorcycle companies was Harley-Davidson. Harley-Davidson became one of the most popular makes of motorcycle.

Classic motorcycles

Classic motorcycles look good as well as feel good to ride.

A classic motorcycle is an old motorcycle that is famous because of the way it looks. The Harley-Davidson 45 is a classic motorcycle. It was made in the 1940s.

Collectors keep their classic motorcycles shiny and in perfect condition.

Many people enjoy collecting classic motorcycles. They spend hours repairing, cleaning, and polishing them. Collectors often display their bikes at classic motorcycle shows.

Where motorcycles are used

Most motorcycles are used on roads that have a smooth surface. Riding a motorcycle is a good way of getting around quickly. Many people use them in busy towns and cities.

In countries where there are many people, motorcycles are useful for driving to work and school.

Motorcycles do not take up much space on a narrow road.

In some places, roads are very narrow. It is hard for cars to drive along these roads. Motorcycles are a good way to get around these places.

Mopeds

A moped is like a bicycle with a small **engine** attached. Mopeds are cheap to buy and easy to use. Riders often use a moped when they are first learning to ride a motorcycle.

Mopeds are smaller than other motorcycles.

pedal

The pedals on a moped
help it to keep up speed.

A moped has pedals like the pedals on a bicycle.
The rider pedals to start the engine. The pedals
also give extra power when going up steep hills.

Scooters

A scooter has much smaller wheels than a normal motorcycle. Many people ride scooters to get to work. In some countries teenagers ride them for fun.

Scooters can be small but they can still carry two people.

engine

The small engine on a scooter means that it is good for going short distances.

A scooter has a small **engine** next to the rear wheel. It makes the rear wheel turn to make the scooter move. The rider's seat is above the engine.

Superbikes

Riders can race against each other on very powerful motorcycles called superbikes. These bikes can whizz along at nearly 300 kilometres (185 miles) per hour.

Superbikes have large engines and they can go very fast.

helmet

knee pad

Riders lean their superbikes over to help them go round corners.

The superbike's wide, rounded **tyres** give plenty of grip to stop it skidding. The riders wear special clothing. They have pads to protect their knees.

Motocross bikes

A motocross bike is used for racing over hilly, bumpy dirt tracks. The riders often slide their feet along the ground. This helps them to stop falling over.

Motocross racing on dirt tracks is a popular sport in some countries.

Motocross bikes have **tyres** with a chunky **tread** that grips well in the muddy ground. The wheels have strong, springy **suspension** for going over bumps and jumps.

suspension

Riders get very dirty while racing and jumping their motocross bikes.

Touring motorcycles

Touring motorcycles are large and comfortable to ride long distances.

Touring motorcycles are for riders who want to go on long journeys. They are big motorcycles. They have an **engine** that is as big and powerful as a car engine.

Panniers can hold clothes and other items so the rider can go on a holiday on the motorcycle.

pannier

At the back of a touring motorcycle is a luggage rack. On the rack there are luggage containers called panniers. There is also an extra seat called a pillion seat for a passenger.

Patrol bikes

Police officers use patrol bikes to get quickly to the scenes of accidents or crimes. They use special touring motorcycles. The motorcycles are fitted with a **two-way radio**.

Police motorcycles are large and fast.

Police patrol bikes have flashing lights and loud **sirens**. The lights and siren warn drivers and **pedestrians** that the bike is coming. This gives people a chance to move out of the way.

Police motorcycles have some of the same equipment as a police patrol car, like radios and flashing lights.

Sidecars

Some motorcycles have a sidecar. A sidecar has a seat for a passenger inside. Together, the motorcycle and the sidecar are called a combination motorcycle.

sidecar

Sidecars allow a motorcycle driver to bring a passenger along.

A sidecar has its own wheel. This means that a combination motorcycle has three wheels. The motorcycle rider on a combination motorcycle cannot lean it over to go round corners.

The passenger in a sidecar can have a fun ride!

Motorcycle taxis

In some countries the streets buzz with three-wheeled motorcycles. They are called rickshaws. Many rickshaws are used as taxis.

Rickshaws have seats for several passengers.

Rickshaws are used in countries such as India.

Most rickshaws are really scooters with two wheels at the back instead of one. They can be easier to drive in crowded areas than a normal taxi. The driver sits at the front and steers using handlebars.

Timeline

1868   Two brothers called Michaux fit a steam **engine** to a
bicycle to make a simple motorcycle.

1885   Two German engineers called Daimler and Maybach
build one of the first motorcycles. It has a small petrol
engine.

1907   The first TT motorcycle races are held on the Isle of Man.
The races are still held today. TT stands for Tourist Trophy.

1950s   The first scooters are built in Italy. They become popular
for teenagers to ride in the 1960s.

1968   The world's first superbike is shown at the Tokyo Motor
Show. It is the Honda CB750.

2006   Denis Manning of the United States breaks the world
record for speed on a specially built motorcycle. He
travels at 564.6 kilometres (350 miles) per hour.

Glossary

engine machine that powers movement using fuel

fuel substance that burns to make heat. Motorcycles use petrol as fuel for their engines.

pedestrian person walking along the side of a road or crossing a road

rubber a soft, flexible material made from chemicals. It is poured into moulds to make tyres.

siren device that makes a loud warning noise. Emergency vehicles have sirens to warn people that they are coming.

suspension system of springs that let a motorcycle's wheels move up and down over bumps

tread pattern of grooves around the outside of a tyre. The tread makes the tyres grip on wet or muddy roads.

two-way radio radio that lets you talk and listen to someone else

tyre rubber ring that fits around the outside of a wheel. It has a chunky tread on the outside and is filled with air.

Find Out More

Machines at Work: Motorcycles, Cynthia Roberts (Child's World, 2007).

Mighty Motorbikes, Chris Oxlade (Franklin Watts, 2006).

Sports Machines: Off-road Motorcycles, E. S. Budd (Child's World, 2006).

World's Greatest Motorbikes, Ian Graham (Raintree, 2005).

Index